AMSTERDAM

THE CITY AT A GL

GW00567975

Westerkerk
From its 85m tower, the 'W
impressive views over gal
Prinsengracht 281, T 624

Stadsschouwburg
The delightful neo-Renais
of the city's most innovative cultural centres.
Leidseplein 26, T 624 2311

Van Gogh Museum
On show in the main building is the artist's
work; temporary exhibitions are housed in
Kisho Kurokawa's 1999 extension.
See p014

Centraal Station
Amsterdam boasts a majestic 19th-century
railway terminal as its primary transport hub.
Stationsplein

Rijksmuseum
Dating from 1885, this museum is where the
nation's Golden Age treasures are displayed.
See p035

Stadsarchief
Designed almost a century ago as a statement
of the might of Dutch international trade, the
building is a symphony in polychromatic brick.
See p010

NEMO
Resembling an ocean tanker, Renzo Piano's
science centre sits on top of the IJtunnel, the
cars-only underwater connection to Noord.
See p013

Hermitage Amsterdam
A branch of the St Petersburg museum, the
Hermitage has become a local arts institution.
Amstel 51, T 530 7488

INTRODUCTION
THE CHANGING FACE OF THE URBAN SCENE

Constructed on a mostly manmade landscape, the Netherlands has, fundamentally, always been about design. Amsterdam, like Venice, is a grand marvel of imagination atop a warren of ancient canals. Unlike its Italian counterpart, however, it is an evolving metropolis and not a bejewelled museum piece. A peek into the uncurtained windows of the 17th-century canal houses lining its four principal waterways says much about the city's psyche. Often modernised, always welcoming, these interiors reveal a cultured, mercantile people of irreverent humour; qualities also displayed by the Dutch designers, like Marcel Wanders, Hella Jongerius and the progeny of Droog, who took the world by storm in the early noughties.

Design continues to merge with every aspect of Amsterdam life. Its pervasiveness is apparent in the latest hotels, clubs, bars and restaurants, as well as on the high street, where department stores like HEMA commission up-and-coming creatives. Similarly, new developments in Noord and the former *havens* involve local artists and architects from the initial stages, resulting in lively, futuristic districts that blur the borders between work and play.

Meanwhile, the government is striving to tame the beasts – sex, drugs and rock 'n' roll – that made this place so infamous. The red-light district is being cleaned up; the legendary coffeeshops and neon windows here are in decline as the capital rebrands itself and high-end restaurants, studios and boutiques enter the mix.

ESSENTIAL INFO
FACTS, FIGURES AND USEFUL ADDRESSES

TOURIST OFFICE
Stationsplein 10
T 702 6000
www.iamsterdam.com

TRANSPORT
Airport transfer to city centre
NS trains depart every 15 minutes from
6am to 1am, hourly from 1am to 5am.
The journey takes 15 minutes
www.ns.nl
Bicycle hire
MacBike
www.macbike.nl
Taxis
Taxicentrale
T 777 7777
Watertaxi
T 535 6363
Travel card
A 72-hour all-zone City Card includes free
entry to most attractions
www.iamsterdam.com

EMERGENCY SERVICES
Emergencies
T 112
Late-night pharmacy (until 10pm)
Leidsestraat Apotheek
Leidsestraat 74-76
T 422 0210

CONSULATES
British Consulate-General
Koningslaan 44
T 704 270 427
www.gov.uk/government/world/
netherlands
US Consulate-General
Museumplein 19
T 575 5309
nl.usembassy.gov

POSTAL SERVICES
Post office
Singel 250
T 900 0990
Shipping
UPS
T 504 0500

BOOKS
Amsterdam: A Brief Life of the City
by Geert Mak (Vintage)
The Amsterdam School by Walter Herfst
(Architectura & Natura)
Dutch Design: A History by Mienke
Simon Thomas (Reaktion Books)
Reproducing Scholten & Baijings
by Louise Schouwenberg (Phaidon)

WEBSITES
Art/Design
www.whatdesigncando.com
Newspaper
www.nrc.nl

EVENTS
Amsterdam Art Weekend
www.amsterdamart.com
Grachtenfestival
www.grachtenfestival.nl

COST OF LIVING
Taxi from Amsterdam Airport
Schiphol to city centre
€45
Cappuccino
€3
Packet of cigarettes
€7
Daily newspaper
€2
Bottle of champagne
€80

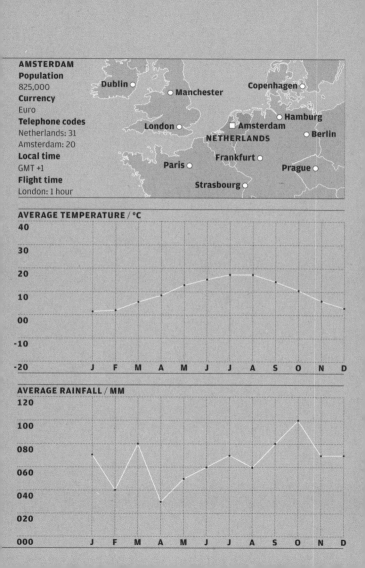

AMSTERDAM
Population
825,000
Currency
Euro
Telephone codes
Netherlands: 31
Amsterdam: 20
Local time
GMT +1
Flight time
London: 1 hour

Dublin Manchester Copenhagen
London Hamburg
Amsterdam Berlin
NETHERLANDS
Paris Frankfurt Prague
Strasbourg

AVERAGE TEMPERATURE / °C

	40	30	20	10	00	-10	-20
	J	F	M	A	M	J	J	A	S	O	N	D

AVERAGE RAINFALL / MM

	120	100	080	060	040	020	000
	J	F	M	A	M	J	J	A	S	O	N	D

NEIGHBOURHOODS
THE AREAS YOU NEED TO KNOW AND WHY

To help you navigate the city, we've chosen the most interesting districts (see below and the map inside the back cover) and colour-coded our featured venues, according to their location; those venues that are outside these areas are not coloured.

DE PIJP

This southern district is one of the most multicultural enclaves in Europe. And since its student and arty residents have been swelled by expats and media types, the area has become extremely happening. The Albert Cuypmarkt has long been an institution, and the streets are lined with cafés (see p044), galleries (see p067) and boutiques (see p092). Also check out the residences around Henriette Ronnerplein, built in the Amsterdam School style.

WESTERPARK

In 2003, when the 19th-century gasworks of Westergasfabriek (Pazzanistraat 33, T 586 0710) was converted into a buzzy arts complex, complete with TV studios, concert venues, a cinema, a theatre, bars and restaurants, the fortunes of this old working-class district began to improve. Within the Westerpark itself, locals come to unwind, picnic, jog and play tennis.

CENTRUM

Amsterdam's notorious red-light district, where the brothels are now partially being replaced by hip restaurants (see p051), is located right in the heart of the city, ringed by the 17th-century Singel, Herengracht, Keizersgracht and Prinsengracht canals. The area is topped by Centraal Station, the capital's impressive neo-Renaissance gateway, and tailed by Stadsarchief (see p010). This is also the prime retail zone; don't miss the iconic Droog (see p093).

JORDAAN

When the aristocracy constructed their elegant canal houses in the 17th century, they also built the Jordaan to accommodate all the craftsmen, brewers, tanners and merchants, and keep them ensconced on the other side of Prinsengracht. For eons, Jordaaners formed a tight community. However, its stylish streets, typified by Brouwersgracht, are now the stomping ground of fashionable thirtysomethings who frequent the bars and restaurants.

HAVENS OOST

The manmade islands of KNSM and Java, and the Borneo Sporenburg peninsulas (see p075), were built as part of the docks and hosted shipping-company offices and warehouses. Today, innovative architecture and state-of-the-art residential projects, such as the impressive bulk of The Whale (see p012), appeal to young families, and the neighbourhood is highly desirable.

OUD ZUID

At the end of the 19th century, Amsterdam expanded rapidly, and Oud Zuid became an important new district. The landscaped green space of Vondelpark prompted the construction of many a mansion, and the cultural playground that is Museumplein now attracts visitors in droves. Among the big-hitting attractions are the Van Gogh Museum (see p014), the Rijksmuseum (see p035) and Stedelijk Museum (see p036), all revamped and back to their very best.

LANDMARKS

THE SHAPE OF THE CITY SKYLINE

Visitors to Amsterdam often long to stay and make it their home. It has everything you could possibly want from a city, including a compact layout that is just right for aimless strolling, and, above all, it offers a simple civic lesson – raise tolerance to the level of principle and, after a time, there will be little need to exercise it.

As with most other northern European cities, it is predicated on the need and desire to be tucked up at home for a good chunk of the year. At the same time, its interiors always seem to be on display to the outside world, and one of its pleasures is not just window-shopping, but window *living*. What must it be like to live in those high-ceilinged apartments on Prinsengracht, with their exquisite lights and minimal decor? Or to gaze out at the canals, which, here and there, reflect the lights hung under the bridges to form magical, sparkling, yellow necklaces? All of which is to say that the capital's charms are discreet ones.

This is one of the world's great walking cities but, unlike in New York or Paris, routes here are seldom marked by a narcissistic tower block or a dominating government structure. If you do want to give your eyes a rest from the gorgeous claustrophobia of the canals, head over to KNSM-eiland, the squeaky-clean eastern dockside development that has taken the concept of a quaint Amsterdam architectural vernacular and blown it right out of the water. *For full addresses, see Resources.*

Stadsarchief
Known as De Bazel, after its architect
Karel, this monumental building was
completed in 1926 for the Netherlands
Trading Company and its striped brick-
and-granite facade is a showpiece of
Dutch expressionism. It now houses the
municipal archive and it's worth a look
for the art deco murals, stained glass,
and exhibitions in vast period rooms.
Vijzelstraat 32, T 251 1511

The Whale

Even among the multitude of new-builds that now make up the Borneo Sporenburg regeneration project, this complex stands out. The size of a football stadium, it squats in the former harbour just like a beached whale, hence its name, and is suitably grey in colour, due to a zinc façade. Designed by Frits van Dongen of architects Cie and completed in 2000, it is one of only three large-scale structures in a part of town where low-rises predominate. The Whale is a sophisticated mixed-use development comprising 214 apartments, 150 of which are social housing; commercial space; an underground car park; and an enclosed courtyard garden, part of which is open to the public. It is elevated on pilotis on two sides and the roof also angles and tilts in order to maximise exposure to sunlight.
Baron GA Tindalplein

NEMO

On top of Renzo Piano's ship-like science museum is a huge sloping stepped terrace, reached via a wide staircase from ground level, conceived as a modern equivalent of the elegant squares in the historic centre. It's just about the only raised public area in this famously flat city and offers a good view back to the old town, which attracts considerable crowds in summer. In spirit, the building, which is surrounded by water on three sides, echoes the massive Borneo Sporenburg docklands rejuvenation, where much of Amsterdam's boldest architecture is situated. When it opened in 1997, it was dismissed by some as 'half a Renzo Piano', because they felt that too many corners had been cut with both the materials and the finish to hit a notoriously tight budget. Gradually, though, it has come to be loved. *Oosterdok 2, T 531 3233, www.e-nemo.nl*

Van Gogh Museum

Japanese architect Kisho Kurokawa had a tough act to follow when he was asked to devise the Van Gogh Museum's exhibition wing: the main building is an understated modern classic designed in the early 1960s by Gerrit Rietveld and opened in 1973. Yet Kurokawa's contribution, finished in 1999, is even more of a crowd-pleaser – still a highlight of the cultural grand prix that is the Museumplein. His asymmetric elliptical building (above), which was rounded off by a glass entrance hall executed by architects Hans van Heeswijk in 2015, does more than stand its ground next to the functionalist original structure. Perhaps the best time to visit is on a Friday night (there are free tours in English at 7pm, open until 10pm), for VJs, music and performing arts events.
Museumplein 6, T 570 5200,
www.vangoghmuseum.nl

HOTELS

WHERE TO STAY AND WHICH ROOMS TO BOOK

Amsterdam is a classic mini-break destination, yet its relatively small size means hotels are often full, especially from March until mid-September. Up until the 1990s, accommodation was limited to numerous grotty hostels, mid-range corporate monoliths and evergreen grandes dames including Amstel (Professor Tulpplein 1, T 622 6060), The Grand (Oudezijds Voorburgwal 197, T 555 3111) and Hotel de l'Europe (Nieuwe Doelenstraat 2-14, T 531 1777).

The 21st-century Dutch design revolution changed all that. The Conservatorium (opposite), Hotel Arena ('s-Gravesandestraat 55, T 850 2400) and Lloyd Hotel (Oostelijke Handelskade 34, T 561 3636) attract a hip and savvy crowd. There was a clamour around the launch of Marcel Wanders' Andaz (Prinsengracht 587, T 523 1234) and Sir Albert (Albert Cuypstraat 2-6, T 305 3020), in an old diamond factory, and now the buzz surrounds the local hospitality group's follow-up Sir Adam (see p020). And since The Hoxton (see p018), Pulitzer (see p026) and Waldorf Astoria (Herengracht 542-556, T 710 6090), featuring a Guerlain Spa and a two-Michelin-starred restaurant (T 718 4643), have also entered the fray, there is serious competition at the highest end. B&Bs are modernising too in the face of a certain home-letting website: try Marcel's Creative Exchange (Leidsestraat 87, T 622 9834) and Stout & Co (see p029). Or go Dutch and rent a houseboat (www.houseboathotel.nl). *For full addresses and room rates, see Resources.*

Conservatorium

Near Museumplein, this hotel, opened in 2011, breathes with appropriately rarefied air. It occupies a 19th-century building that was once home to a music conservatory, with soaring ceilings that enabled Piero Lissoni to renovate nearly half of the 129 rooms as duplexes (Grand Duplex Suite, above). Melding contemporary design with classic luxury, interiors are a mellow blend of wood, glass and metal, and some rooms feature original pinewood beams. Kick back in the brasserie, on the terrace in summer, or at the Asian-inspired restaurant Taiko by Schilo, whose calling card is to make inventive use of a core ingredient every season. Another major draw is the Akasha Holistic Wellbeing Centre (T 570 0067), for its Watsu pool and hammam treatments. *Van Baerlestraat 27, T 570 0000, www.conservatoriumhotel.com*

The Hoxton

When this hotel, located between two of the city's prestigious waterways, reopened as part of The Hoxton chain in 2015, a dose of Golden Age flair was re-established. It is set in a warren-like fusion of five stately merchant houses, including the former mayor's residence. Local studio Nicemakers have doused the 111 rooms in gentlemanly style, favouring materials that age well, like the oak floors, a deep blue, sea green, tan and ochre palette, and mirrors designed in collaboration with David Derksen and Lex Pott, as seen in the Floral Room 107 (right). Judging by the competition for real estate on the velvet armchairs and Chesterfields in the lounge, The Hoxton has succeeded in its secondary mission of creating a home from home for the local MacBook-wielding types, who are kept in avocado and eggs by the all-day brasserie Lotti's (T 888 5500). *Herengracht 255, T 888 5555, www.thehoxton.com/amsterdam*

Sir Adam

Get past the annoying conceit that you're the guest of a playboy aristocrat, and Sir Adam is a welcome addition to Noord. It is part of A'DAM Toren, a 2016 conversion of a 1971 tower designed by Arthur Staal for Royal Dutch Shell. Its 22 storeys now house hip music firms, a techno club, a revolving restaurant and a cantilevered rooftop deck set at 45 degrees. On the first eight floors, Sir Adam's 108 rooms (Sir Suite 711, above) all have floor-to-ceiling windows, even in some of the marble bathrooms. Manhattan interior design firm Icrave have taken their cue from the concrete skeleton to create a loft vibe, installing Gibson guitars (on the walls) and Crosley Cruiser turntables. There is a vinyl library in the lobby (opposite), as well as happening canteen The Butcher. *Overhoeksplein 7, T 215 9500, www.sirhotels.com/adam*

Hotel V Fizeaustraat

Eyebrows were raised when the V chain, which already had popular shabby-chic properties on Nesplein (T 662 3233) and Frederiksplein (T 662 3233), opened a larger venture in off-radar Amsteldorp in 2016. Yet V Fizeaustraat became its crowning glory, with the legendary Piet Zanstra's brutalist 1970s office block an ideal canvas for Mirjam Espinosa's retro vision. Plenty of oak and lush textiles in green and brown soften the space, and the 91 rooms have the right balance of vintage quirk – tie-dye wallpaper – and mod cons, such as Dornbracht showers. The atmospheric Lobby restaurant (T 758 5275; pictured) has helped enormously, as chef Jeroen van Spall's pan-European menu pulls locals from the city centre. *Fizeaustraat 2, T 662 3233.* *www.hotelvfizeaustraat.nl*

The Dylan

This boutique bolthole was revamped in 2006 by local interiors studio FG Stijl, who gave it a sleek overhaul while retaining its exquisite spirit. Today, each of the 40 rooms and suites have a distinctive style and colour scheme; our favourite is the white, orchid-bedecked Loft Suite (above), due to its original timber beams. In 2014, the Serendipity Collection was unveiled: 16 accommodations by Dutch architect and designer Remy Meijers, renowned for his stripped-back, tranquil vision, which has proved a perfect match for The Dylan's understated luxury. It is worth dining at either of the in-house eateries – Brasserie OCCO or the Michelin-starred Restaurant Vinkeles, renowned for delicate, seasonal, French-led cuisine – alongside the black polo neck and shades brigade, who bring with them an air of glamorous intrigue. *Keizersgracht 384, T 530 2010, www.dylanamsterdam.com*

Pulitzer

This sprawling multi-canal-house hotel had a post-Starwood-divorce makeover in 2016 and is looking ravishing. It was led by South African Jacu Strauss, who opted for a rich mustard-and-blue palette inspired by the hues in Vermeer's *The Milkmaid*. Many of the furnishings were custom-designed, and there are patchwork Persian rugs by Piet Hein Eek. The 225 unique pads come with various eccentric amenities such as a vintage telephone and a minibar with cocktail-mixing facilities. Its four grandest reservations take a theme and run away with it, from the Book Collector's Suite, featuring a floor-to-ceiling arch of vintage tomes, to the Art Collector's Suite (above), which leaves little to the imagination. The romantic garden courtyard is a lovely spot. *Prinsengracht 315-331, T 523 5235, www.pulitzeramsterdam.com*

CitizenM

'Never, ever underestimate the pillow.'
That's one of the founding principles of
local firm Concrete's prefabricated hotel
concept, part of a wider manifesto stating
that affordability and indulgence should
not be mutually exclusive. The rooms,
the shells of which are made in a factory
off-site, have something of the space pod
about them, and come with a touchpad
that can adjust everything from lighting
to the blinds and the flat-screen TV. The
welcoming lobby (above) is fully decked
out with Vitra eye candy including a Hella
Jongerius 'Polder' sofa, and the bookcase
is stacked with design publications. For a
venue with an ominous-looking automated
check-in booth, there is a quite reassuring
number of staff on hand to help.
Prinses Irenestraat 30, T 811 7090,
www.citizenm.com

Zoku

Like CitizenM (see p027), Zoku is another innovative idea executed by Concrete that will appeal far beyond its mothership. The 133 'lofts' in this huge building off what has been coined 'knowledge mile' by the start-up-crazed government are home/office units in five sizes, from 16 to 46 sq m. By making a working table and not the bed the focus, and allowing for the vanishing of sleeping quarters by way of retractable steps and slatted wood doors, the rooms (XL, above) feel appropriate for meetings, and each floor has an art library that lends out cheerful prints for the walls. Up on the green roof, Social Spaces is an airy lounge for work and play beside the day members who pay a fee to hotdesk here, and Living Kitchen serves lavish, salad-heavy spreads. *Weesperstraat 105, T 811 2811, www.livezoku.com*

Stout & Co

Interior designer Stefan Bennebroek and landscape architect Steven Delva have created their own intricate universe in a functionalist 1956 college building on the foundations of a former brewery. Their studios are on the ground floor, and they live in the penthouse up top. In-between, a breakfast lounge and six suites line up along a lush terrace. Placing an emphasis on original fixtures, the accommodation (Mixed Green, above) has separate sleeping and kitchen areas, and the furnishings are designed by the owners or their friends, such as the Belgian creative platform De Invasie, who also supplied some of the art. This attention to detail extends to Aesop toiletries and the cards that list the duo's recommendations of local bars and shops. *Hoogte Kadijk 71, T 220 9071, www.stout-co.com*

Maison Rika
Swedish stylist-turned-designer Ulrika
Lundgren opened this two-suite spot in
an 18th-century building across the road
from her boutique (see p080) in 2011.
Here she combines the original wooden
floors and beams with contemporary art.
The corner Loft Room (pictured) affords
a view over the Herengracht canal and
De Negen Straatjes shopping district.
Oude Spiegelstraat 12, T 330 1112

24 HOURS
SEE THE BEST OF THE CITY IN JUST ONE DAY

It's an oft-repeated local joke that Amsterdam has four seasons in one day. Truth be told, conditions are generally mild, if changeable, but people have to find something to complain about in a city with a quality of life that is ranked among the best on the planet.

No trip would be complete without exploring the Canal Belt, either by bicycle or on a cruise (www.water-taxi.nl). Amsterdam came into its own as a global trade and shipbuilding capital in the 1600s, giving rise to the extravagant merchant houses and artistic treasures of the Golden Age – see the Old Masters at Rembrandthuis (Jodenbreestraat 4, T 520 0400) and the Rijksmuseum (see p035), stopping for lunch in-between at a canal-side café such as Buffet van Odette (Prinsengracht 598, T 423 6034). Spend the afternoon delving into the contemporary art scene (see p064), including the photo gallery Foam (Keizersgracht 609, T 551 6500); old churches Oude Kerk (Oudekerksplein 23, T 625 8284) and De Nieuwe Kerk (Dam Square, T 638 6909) also host atmospheric exhibitions.

Until the late 20th century, the Dutch wanted little more on their plate other than meat, potatoes and cheese. But immigration has brought innumerable culinary advances and the diversity is now dazzling, particularly on Kinkerstraat, exemplified by Seoul Food (No 73a, T 331 8843). To taste local inventiveness and provenance, you should not miss De Kas (see p038) and Hangar (see p055). *For full addresses, see Resources.*

09.00 Bocca

Although its notoriety for the other sort of coffeeshop endures, the Dutch love a cup of joe, and the city has succumbed to the artisanal uprising. Since 2015, obsessives have been rocking up to this light-flooded former car mechanic's to quiz the baristas on strengths and grinding techniques. The equipment takes centre stage, notably the four-group La Marzocco Strada espresso machine. Dotted about are 1950s velvet armchairs, 'Acapulco' chairs, a sardine-can cabinet and a rebar and Dutch elm shelving unit stacked with brewing paraphernalia and bags of coffee to take home. Brothers Menno and Tewis Simons now supply their bespoke roasts to hundreds of businesses across the country. The homemade vegan treats, including carrot cake and banana bread, are a semi-virtuous start to the day.
Kerkstraat 96, T 321 314 667, www.bocca.nl

11.30 Moooi

In Moooi — the Dutch word for 'beautiful' with an extra 'o' — Marcel Wanders and co-founder Casper Vissers, who left after 14 years in 2015, have built a flamboyant protagonist of the Amsterdam design scene in less than two decades. It now draws on a collective of around 30 individuals, from local upstarts such as Joost van Bleiswijk, Frank Tjepkema and Bertjan Pot, to global names like Nika Zupanc and Neri & Hu.

Always novel, and often eccentric, Moooi's classics include Raimond Puts' celestial lights (above), comprising two lattice-steel spheres separated by LEDs, and Maarten Baas' gothic 'Smoke' series, made from resin-protected burnt wood. More luggage-friendly is Wanders' 'The Killing of the Piggy Bank' vase. Closed Sundays and Mondays. *Westerstraat 187, T 528 7760, www.moooi.com*

14.00 Rijksmuseum

The mantra for Spanish firm Cruz y Ortiz's restoration of the 1885 Rijksmuseum was 'continue with Cuypers', the Dutchman who designed the 'nation's treasure house'. This meant removing postwar interventions to two internal patios, whose floors were sunk to form a vast atrium (above); returning the library to its original state; and adding a new sandstone and glass pavilion set in water to display ancient Asian art. Queues are endless, so book online to view the 80 rooms showing 8,000 pieces, among them Rembrandt's *Night Watch*, Vermeer's *The Milkmaid* and Van Gogh's 1887 *Self-portrait*, and period decorative arts and furniture. However, for locals, the pearl is the vaulted bike path that, due to lobbying, continues to pass straight through the museum. *Museumstraat 1, T 674 7000, www.rijksmuseum.nl*

16.00 Stedelijk Museum

In 2012, after a nine-year renovation, the Stedelijk was ready to regain its spot as one of the world's top contemporary art and design museums. The distinctive shape and texture of the smooth, white, polyester-resin wing (pictured) added by Benthem Crouwel, with its glass-encased ground floor and cantilevered roof, led to it being dubbed 'the bathtub'. It hosts temporary exhibitions, which under the stewardship of Beatrix Ruf have often been headline multimedia shows, and abuts the 19th-century neo-Renaissance original. Here, the permanent collection of more than 90,000 pieces from 1870 to now includes classic Dutch works such as Mondrian's *Tableau III* and De Kooning's *Rosy-Fingered Dawn at Louse Point*. *Museumplein 10, T 573 2911, www.stedelijk.nl*

19.30 De Kas

Deep in the east of Amsterdam, this 1926 greenhouse is home to a restaurant which, since 2001, has steadily become the city's forerunner of all that is locally produced and sourced. The daily Mediterranean-inspired set menus are based around fresh vegetables and herbs, harvested at sunrise by founder and owner Gert Jan Hageman in an adjoining garden and nearby nursery. These ingredients are matched with the best of what De Kas' sustainable suppliers have to offer. Past dishes include cucumber gazpacho with melon, marinated mackerel and chives, lamb chop with edible-flower salad, and roasted loin of veal with braised radicchio, Hollandaise sauce and anchovy jus. Lunch is served on weekdays only, and on the patio in summer. Closed Sundays. *Kamerlingh Onneslaan 3, T 462 4562, www.restaurantdekas.nl*

URBAN LIFE

CAFÉS, RESTAURANTS, BARS AND NIGHTCLUBS

The dining scene in Amsterdam is a cyclical affair. Once the bulbs bloom in May, the *nieuwe haring* (new herring) season begins and locals indulge in their answer to sashimi, garnished with gherkins and bought from street stalls. The roads lining the canals evoke a Continental café scene, where open sandwiches and *witbier* are par for the course. At the height of summer, the terrace of the spaceship-esque 't Blauwe Theehuis (Vondelpark 5, T 662 0254), and urban beaches Amsterdam Roest (Jacob Bontiusplaats 1, T 308 0283) and Hannekes Boom (Dijksgracht 4, T 419 9820) are packed.

There is no end of quirky sit-down places too, from an art deco cinema (see p044) to a morgue (see p054) and a tram shed (see p059). Equally offbeat, Restaurant As (Prinses Irenestraat 19, T 644 0100) occupies a chapel, REM Eiland (Haparandadam 45-2, T 688 5501) sits atop an oil rig, and De School (Dr Jan van Breemenstraat 1, T 737 3197) now hosts cultural happenings and club nights. This city is always up for a party, of course. Café Brecht (Weteringschans 157, T 627 2211) is popular before a night out around Leidseplein, to catch a live gig at Paradiso (Weteringschans 6-8, T 626 4521) or Melkweg (Lijnbaansgracht 234a, T 531 8181), or dance at Chicago Social Club (No 12, T 760 1171). At weekends, head over to Canvas (Wibautstraat 150, T 261 2110), on top of the former De Volkskrant building, to bop until it's time to watch the sunrise from the terrace. *For full addresses, see Resources.*

Wyers

San Francisco's Kimpton Hotels made its European debut in 2017 with the anodyne De Witt near the station. More of a hit is Wyers, its moody, masculine eaterie, with portraits by Dutch photographer Maarten Schröder hung on weathered plaster walls, intimate booths, parquet flooring, Hans J Wegner 'Elbow' chairs, a wood and marble bar and an industrial-looking ceiling. The all-day menu centres on US comfort fare, with breakfasts of pancakes with syrup, or beignets (pastry fritters) made to order at next-door café Miss Louisa (T 521 1755). At lunch and weekend brunch, there is a Reuben sandwich, lobster roll, Cobb salad and burritos. Chef Sam DeMarco shows his finesse at dinner with mains like chicken 'puttanesca' with smoked eel and escarole. *Kimpton de Witt, Nieuwendijk 60, T 521 1755, www.restaurantwyers.com*

De Tropen

Muted green paintwork and dark marble surfaces keep the references the right side of caricature in this sophisticated dining and drinking haunt, where windows open onto the Oosterpark. It is part of the Royal Tropical Institute complex that includes the Tropenmuseum, which examines the relationship between the Netherlands and the world at large, with specific reference to colonialism. Local design studio Piet Boon has been sympathetic to the original 1926 structure, a Gothic revival mansion by JJ Van Nieukerken intended to promote trade throughout all the Dutch territories, and the expansive terrace has proved to be a hit with Oost's bright young things. The kitchen serves up imaginative global fusion dishes under the mantra 'eat together'.
Linnaeusstraat 2, T 568 2000, www.amsterdamdetropen.nl

CT Coffee and Coconuts

The final curtain may have fallen on this building's former life as a theatre but the drama plays on in its cavernous interior, a rarity in De Pijp. The gorgeous restored 1921 concrete facade by architects Willem Noorlander and Gerrit van Arkel melds the Amsterdam School with proto art deco in its ziggurat form, torch-like lights, stained glass and stylised lettering. Inside, it has been given a breezy cabana-style revamp over three staggered levels under a 12m-high ceiling, with exposed brick, furniture by local makers Sukha, rope and wicker features. Come for the filling breakfasts and comfort food; bespoke espresso from Bocca (see p033); coconut juice flavoured with a splash of lime; and the house beer Dodo, produced by microbrewery Oedipus. *Ceintuurbaan 282-284, T 354 1104, www.coffeeandcoconuts.com*

Choux

Chef Merijn van Berlo and natural wine nut Figo van Onna trialled several successful temporary ventures before settling on the ground floor of Spring House, a members' community of creative and socially minded entrepreneurs. Set on the IJ waterfront, it was a tin can factory before becoming a genever distillery in the 1940s. Designers Müller Van Tol exposed the pipework and introduced scarlet accents that echo the red facade, and a wooden wall installation that's a nod to Choux's pop-up past. There are two seasonal 'vegetable forward' chef's menus of five and seven courses, or go à la carte. We'd return for the crab salad rolled in broccoli leaves with white currants, trout eggs and nasturtium, or the wild duck fillet and liver with blackberries and cavolo nero. *De Ruyterkade 128, T 210 3090, www.choux.nl*

C Amsterdam

The C-word of choice in Masterchef judge Michiel van der Eerde's 2015 restaurant is 'Celsius'. Artfully plated dishes like cheek of veal foie gras arrive with an explanation of cooking conditions (pork belly Hoisin, for example, is prepared overnight sous-vide at 75°C). Like many other new attractions on Wibautstraat, C is in an old newspaper office, and Studio Noun and &Prast&Hooft have collaborated on juxtaposing the shell with high-gloss elements. Copper 'Melt' lamps by Tom Dixon hang above curvy velvet banquettes in the bar (above), and the main space features brass, steel, wood and concrete, pendant lights made from repurposed gas canisters, and graffiti art by Pipsqueak. The 16 counter seats by the open kitchen are great for solo travellers. *Wibautstraat 125, T 210 3011, www.c.amsterdam*

Bar Botanique
The 3WO group is proving that Oost is not the wrong side of the tracks, with funky cocktail joint Bar Bukowski (T 370 1685), artist-themed Bar Basquiat (T 370 8334) and Bar Botanique, a diner with a neat line in G&Ts that opened in 2016. It's a joyous design by Studio Modijefsky, a busy, colourful, double-height interior featuring geometric and organic motifs.
Eerste van Swindenstraat 581, T 358 6553

Café Panache

Daan Bonsen and Leonardo Belloni, whose former glories include gig, art and event space De Marktkantine (T 723 1760), have delivered again here. Designer Will Erens has gone to town (namely, New York City) and he's done an excellent job in evoking Manhattan's Meatpacking District. From walls of salvaged wood crates to clusters of birdcage-like plywood lampshades and plants potted in reclaimed fire station buckets, there is rather a lot going on inside this windowless cocktail bar/grill. Dirk Mooren and Cas van de Pol's menu changes daily, taking advantage of the seasonal produce from the adjacent Ten Kate market. However, seafood platters, catch-of-the-day fish and the signature 800g côte de boeuf are stalwarts. *Ten Katestraat 117, T 221 1736, www.cafepanache.nl*

Restaurant Anna

When this high-end venture launched in 2011 across a pair of imposing 18th-century buildings, it was a sure sign that the red-light district was getting a clean-up. It has now been joined by Mata Hari (T 205 0919), a living-room-style bar with mismatched furniture and a good wine list, and Quartier Putain (T 895 0162), a hipster coffeehouse that shares premises with music label Top Notch. Anna is all wooden floors, exposed brick and copper pendants. In 2016, chef Ben van Geelen took over, introducing the brand of meaty poshed-up peasant food that made his tenure at A La Ferme (since closed) such a solid success. It is typified by dishes like Iberico pork chop with sweet potato, hanger steak with ratatouille, and gnocchi with tenderloin and morel sauce. *Warmoesstraat 111, T 428 1111, www.restaurantanna.nl*

SLA

Meaning 'lettuce' in Dutch, SLA proffers organic, often locally sourced salads, put together to order or following a tried and true combination (such as the carrot and white bean). If all this sounds too healthy, forgo the fresh juices and opt for a craft beer or two from Utrecht organic brewers De Leckere. The interior is another hit by eco-friendly studio Nicemakers (see p018). *Westerstraat 34, T 370 2733*

Strangelove in LAB111

LAB111 — a former morgue by the canal in Oud West — is a harmonious synthesis of the Dutch approach to making ends meet while fostering creativity. Upstairs in this handsome 1917 Amsterdam School pile, adorned with sculptures by the legendary Hildo Krop, are artists' studios and ateliers, while the lower levels house an excellent indie cinema and Strangelove, a pleasingly airy brasserie transformed by architects Vens, who are based in the building. The tiles and restored medical machinery (like the examination light, which was found in the basement) give it a distinct sciency feel. A brilliantly diverse crowd come for chef Dennis Lee's twist on European classics, featuring locally sourced ingredients, as well as Friday drinks and weekend brunch. *Arie Biemondstraat 111, T 616 9994, www.strangelove-amsterdam.nl*

Hangar

Former soap- and popstar Tim Immers' debut on the dining scene was the Italian-inspired hangout Bar Moustache (T 428 1074) in Utrechtsestraat. In 2015, he tried his hand in edgier Noord. With celebrity swagger, he had the nerve to open Hangar next to Hotel de Goudfazant (see p062), the venerable Dutch/French restaurant that brought warehouse dining to the city. While Goudfazant is hip and monumental,

Hangar is backstage and cosy, thanks to a scheme its interior designer Stella Willing has called 'a beautiful mess': a patchwork of green, white and rusty corrugated iron. On the menu are dishes such as Groningen mozzarella with wild tomatoes, and garlic-marinated guinea fowl. At night, the venue throws candlelight out over the waterfront. *Aambeeldstraat 36, T 363 8657, www.hangar.amsterdam*

Morgan & Mees
A handsome 1880s red-brick orphanage
was overhauled into this charming nine-
room hotel in 2015 by designer Marius
Haverkamp. Pop by for a cocktail or the
mod Med cuisine in the brasserie, with
its herringbone floors, chandeliers by
Tonone and local art. If you're lucky with
the weather, there's a lovely courtyard.
Tweede Hugo de Grootstraat 2-6.
T 233 4930. www.morganandmees.com

De Culinaire Werkplaats

Combining a culinary laboratory, a design studio and a restaurant, this Westerpark establishment is a herbivore's heaven. The menu, titled 'eat inspirations', translates into an ever-changing sequence of dishes contextualised by Marjolein Wintjes and cooked by Eric Meursing. The bright space, divided into rooms linked by a patio, is a relaxed yet state-of-the-art platform for the owners' ingenious experiments, such as 'rainproof', comprising artichokes, field peas, black beans, beetroot, violets, green leaves and vene cress; and a marinated turnip and olive oil cake with black fruit and liquorice cress. Wintjes and Meursing leave it to guests to pay what they think the meal is worth. Open Thursday to Saturday, 7pm to 11pm; Sunday, 1pm to 10pm.
Fannius Scholtenstraat 10, T 654 646 576, www.deculinairewerkplaats.nl

Kanarie Club

The 2014 rebirth of a derelict tram depot in residential Oud West into De Hallen, a food, fashion, craft and culture hub, has transformed the area, due in large part to its wildly popular gourmet market. Within the vast complex, Kanarie Club is a brightly coloured work/play haven serving global fare. Designed by Studio Modijefsky, the steel arches of the raised bar pay homage to tram rails, the custom-made furniture resembles carriage seats, the graphics are retro, and there's no end of handy charging sockets, lockers and USB ports, as well as a printer and a photobooth. The mezzanine Pool Bar is a nod to the former squatters who made a water feature out of the rain that leaked through the roof. It serves craft G&Ts and cocktails until late at weekends. *Bellamyplein 51, T 218 1775, www.kanarieclub.nl*

Wilde Zwijnen

This airy space in up-and-coming Oost is cut through with a skylight and simply furnished with hanging plants, reclaimed school chairs and distressed brick walls. The name translates as 'wild boars' and there is a signature stew, but otherwise the contemporary Dutch cuisine is less focused on porcine fare and more about locally sourced organic ingredients, often in unusual combinations. Dishes change regularly but look out for the sauerkraut soup; mullet with smoked potato fritters, oxheart cabbage and samphire; and leg of lamb with shank croquette and carrot mousse. In 2015 the restaurant spawned next-door Eetbar (T 354 4000), a cosier setting that serves season-driven small plates like rabbit paté with kohlrabi salad.
Javaplein 23, T 463 3043,
www.wildezwijnen.com

INSIDERS' GUIDE

ANDREA TRIMARCHI AND SIMONE FARRESIN, DESIGNERS

Italian-born product and furniture design duo Formafantasma (www.formafantasma.com) have worked in the Netherlands for a decade. 'Amsterdam is well connected,' says Trimarchi. 'Its size is manageable yet there is a vibrant design scene. And it is built on water, which makes it special and charming.' They operate out of an old Noord factory, which Farresin loves for 'completely Dutch phenomena such as De Ceuvel, an on-land harbour populated by hippies'. They suggest a sundowner at its Café de Ceuvel (Korte Papaverweg 4, T 229 6210) and more people-watching at warehouse restaurant Hotel de Goudfazant (Aambeeldstraat 10, T 636 5170).

In town, they organise meetings in the garden courtyard of the Pulitzer (see p026). A craving for Italian cuisine might lead them to Bussia (Reestraat 28-32, T 627 8794) for an 'excellent risotto', says Trimarchi, or chic Toscanini (Lindengracht 75, T 623 2813). Rijks (Museumstraat 2, T 674 7555), next to the museum (see p035), is another firm favourite. 'It takes classic ingredients and prepares them in a contemporary way,' says Farresin. For culture, the duo praise the 'visionary' approach of director Beatrix Ruf at the Stedelijk Museum (see p036) and check out artwork by their peers at Fons Welters (see p068). They often socialise at De School (see p040), which has swallowed up many a weekend. Trimarchi says: 'We like the various areas, and the club always has great DJs.' *For full addresses, see Resources.*

ART AND DESIGN

GALLERIES, STUDIOS AND PUBLIC SPACES

When a pair of stolen masterpieces were returned to the Van Gogh Museum (see po14) in 2017 after 14 years in gangland Italy, it felt like the symbolic final chapter in the reversal of the city's fortunes. Half a decade earlier, the fanfare reopenings on the Museumplein were muted by concern about the effect of budget cuts and evictions on smaller fish. But now, artistic *broedplaatsen* ('breeding grounds'), cheap premises in mixed-use buildings, exemplified by LAB111 (see po54), have picked up the slack. And established gallerists like Ron Mandos (Prinsengracht 282, T 320 70336) believe that blockbuster shows in the major venues are pulling exciting rising stars back into the indie arena. For experimental work, visit W139 (Warmoesstraat 139, T 622 9434) or De Appel (Schipluidenlaan 12, T 625 5651).

The Dutch heritage as a wealthy trading nation, whose instinct towards ostentation was always tempered by Calvinism, gave rise to a design aesthetic that can be broadly characterised as pared back with flashes of humour – see the jaunty utility of Droog (see po93). Today, the scene is not so much about tasteful sofas but socially conscious initiatives, typified by 'Dream Out Loud', a 2016 group exhibition at Stedelijk (see po36), for which Amsterdam's Studio Drift created covetable mirrors using chemical waste, and projects like 3D Print Canal House and MX3D Bridge, which test techniques that could be applied remotely to build disaster-relief shelters. *For full addresses, see Resources.*

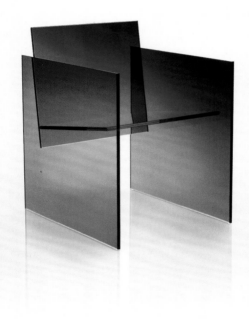

Germans Ermičs

Latvian-born Germans Ermičs approaches colour as a constituent material, rather than simply decoration, and saturates his glasswork creations in graded hues. His output includes tables, consoles, mirrors, room dividers and chromatic display units, as can be seen at Raf Simons' Dover Street Market concession in London. At Salone del Mobile in 2017 he unveiled a tribute to Shiro Kuramata's 1976 'Glass Chair', which distils form into near incorporeality. For his 'Ombré' chair (above), Ermičs deployed the same light-activated adhesive, but instead of transparent glass, he used variegated sheets that overlap to produce iridescence: 'A perception of colour flowing through as if it were liquid,' he says. Bespoke pieces can be commissioned at his studio, which he set up here in 2014; appointment only. *www.germansermics.com*

P/////Akt

Artists are asked to produce work from scratch at this bleeding-edge non-profit gallery, which since 2003 has become a must-visit thanks to its inspired quirkiness ('Daisy Chain' by Lorelinde Verhees, above). You may well happen across an artist in the flesh – sculptor Evita Vasiljeva's 2017 exhibition was the result of two months of on-site moulding and casting. A smaller area up an iron spiral staircase champions graduates, many of whom have gone on to bigger things; for example, Saskia Noor van Imhoff, whose beautiful installations meld sculpture, photography and daily objects. The warehouse space is nestled in a row of car-repair garages in the east docks, where amiable founders Nienke Vijlbrief and Rob van de Werdt throw lively opening parties. *Zeeburgerpad 53, T 654 270 879, www.pakt.nu*

Grimm

Art dealer Jorg Grimm knocked together a bicycle showroom and two neighbouring units in 2010 to form this impressive venue. His métier is steering mid-career artists to greater renown, and he has secured six-figure sums for their oeuvre. The globally minded stable includes US artist Jonathan Marshall, whose intriguing pieces appear to have withstood time ('...More Remnants of Futures Past', above), while homegrown charges are conceptual art pioneer Ger van Elk, famous for his rope sculptures, and photographer Dana Lixenberg, who documents the fringes of society. Grimm has a more intimate, central setting in a Keizersgracht townhouse that hosts mini solo exhibitions, such as six works by New Leipzig School painter Matthias Weischer. *Frans Halsstraat 26, T 675 2465, www.grimmgallery.com*

Galerie Fons Welters
Since opening in a former garage back
in 1988, Welters has built a reputation
for nurturing local talent, with a focus
on abstract sculpture and installation,
encapsulated by Job Koelewijn's text-
based 'Higher Contradictions' (pictured),
conveying a sense of language in flux.
A versatile area by the entrance presents
solo exhibitions by the latest hotshots.
Bloemstraat 140, T 423 3046

Cuyperspassage

Local architects Benthem Crouwel's 110m-long pedestrian and cycle tunnel under Centraal Station was unveiled in 2015 as part of its modernisation. The decorative masterstroke is Irma Boom Office's ceramic tableau all along the length of the raised footpath. Royal Tichelaar Makkum spent five years making and glazing 46,000 wall tiles, as well as 33,000 for the floor, in the traditional 13 sq cm size. On the old-town side, a Delft blue naval scene was inspired by a work by Golden Age painter Cornelis Boumeester, featuring a warship, merchant vessels, the herring fleet, high waves and swooping gulls. It gradually morphs into an abstract pixelated assemblage towards the Noord end. The bike lane, used by up to 15,000 riders daily, is finished in sound-absorbing material and delineated by LEDs. *Stationsplein*

Looiersgracht 60

This low-key but fascinating not-for-profit enterprise investigates the intersection between different disciplines, with a focus on art, design and architecture ('Africa Junctions' by Lard Buurman, above). It hosts thought-provoking solo exhibitions, including work that is often site-specific, within an 1850 cardboard factory, and later beer bottling plant, that was adapted by architect Moriko Kira and opened in 2013.

The hulking elevator, cast-iron grating and peeling posters were retained, and true to Japanese principles, the new poured floor was finished a respectful distance from the original elements. Shows are accompanied by desirable publicity material created by Studio Veronica Ditting, including a limited-edition series of bespoke pocket books.
Looiersgracht 60, T 772 8006,
www.looiersgracht60.org

ARCHITOUR

A GUIDE TO AMSTERDAM'S ICONIC BUILDINGS

Contemporary Dutch architecture is among the most innovative in Europe, but Amsterdam will always have a split personality, its canal-side vernacular of gables and big windows contrasting with nonconformist recent buildings. Exciting new projects roll on, such as the mixed-use IJdock development at Westerdokseiland; the overhaul of the Rijksmuseum (see p035) by Cruz y Ortiz; and Maccreanor Lavington's revamp of the Kraaiennest metro station (Karspeldreef), which has a laser-cut floral facade. After flirting with modernist tendencies in the early 20th century through the Amsterdam School, the city decided it was managing nicely with existing traditions, but visitors who venture away from the historic centre may be surprised. In the east, urban renewal at Het Funen, notably Verdana (Funenpark 360-369) by architects NL, provides evidence of creative residential design, and the Zuidas area proves corporate initiatives can have character too – remarkable buildings here include the UNStudio Tower (Gustav Mahlerlaan 14). Also well worth seeing is ING House (Amstelveenseweg 500) by MVSA.

When KNSM, the last of the city's shipping giants, tanked in 1977, Havens Oost (see p075) was earmarked for a rebirth. Unlike most docklands schemes, though, this one was aimed at aesthetes and involved almost every architect in town; the resulting avant-garde interpretation of classic tract housing signalled a welcome change. *For full addresses, see Resources.*

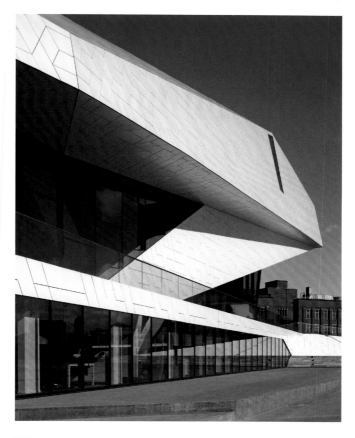

EYE

Opened in 2012, the home of the EYE film institute, designed by architects Delugan Meissl Associated, resembles a bird about to take flight. Situated in the once-forlorn Noord, a free two-minute ferry ride from the rear of Centraal Station, EYE contains small pods in which up to three people at a time can dip into its extensive archives in order to screen a world-class collection of films. In addition, contemporary arthouse fare and classics from celebrated auteurs can be enjoyed in the four cinemas, one of which evokes an old Parisian-style theatre. Together with Tolhuistuin (T 763 0650), an arts and music venue, and, further west, the NDSM (Tt Neveritaweg 15), a shipyard-turned-creative-complex, EYE is just one of several reasons to cross the IJ these days. *IJpromenade 1, T 589 1400, www.eyefilm.nl*

De Piramides

The distinctive silhouette of this apartment block from 2006 was intended by architect Sjoerd Soeters to echo the 17th-century Canal Belt's stepped gables, which served as a way of identifying houses (by crest or shape) before reliable numbering. This system is emblematic of how Amsterdam has long embraced form and function. At 55m high, the towers are a commanding presence in a low-rise part of town. The building forms a continuous whole up until the 11th floor, at which point it splits in two. It's only when you get up closer that you realise the two halves are staggered, by roughly the depth of one flat. The design enables multiple balconies on both sides. In the age of Instagram, local wags have likened De Piramides to a certain smiling brown emoji. There's no planning for that.

Jan van Galenstraat 1-29

Hope, Love and Fortune

Part of the redevelopment of Havens Oost docklands, Borneo Sporenburg is largely residential, but even if you can't wangle an invite (or book an Airbnb), come to admire this 2002 winner of the national prize for sustainable architecture, designed by Rudy Uytenhaak. The three separate blocks are connected by a huge cascading Norwegian marble facade that forms a clear boundary between the private homes and the public park. Created in collaboration with Dutch artist Willem Oorebeek, the lattice screen is covered with black ceramic dots on its undersides, which play with the perception of depth. It's named after a trio of windmills that used to stand here. Nearby, also check out the National Maritime Museum's glass atrium roof (T 523 2222) by Ney & Partners, inspired by compass lines on ocean charts. *Rietlandterras 2-54*

Floating Houses, IJburg

A trio of artificial islands in the east, IJburg was an audacious plan to alleviate the city's housing shortage. Construction began in 1996, residents first arrived in 2002, and it now accommodates 10,000 pioneers. Built on a shipyard in 2011 and transported here by tug, the 75 homes in the floating enclave of Waterbuurt West (above) were designed by Marlies Rohmer. The triangular shape of the allotment was dictated by the diagonal slicing of the basin by power lines, and the layout appears informal, although units are linked by walkways and jetties for docking boats. The three-storey steel modules are stabilised by a submerged concrete 'tub', and are easily customised by alternating glazing and panelling. They are fascinating for their palpably Dutch fusion of romance, utilitarianism and mastery of water.
Waterbuurt West, Steigereiland

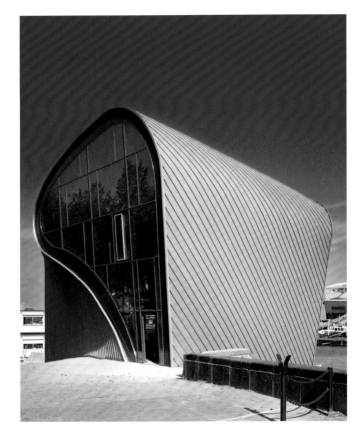

ARCAM

Completed in 2003, and still looking as if it is a vision of some alternative future, the Amsterdam Centre for Architecture should be the first stop in any architour of the capital. Created as an information point for buildings both old and new, it hosts provocative lectures, exhibitions and discussions. We recommend picking up one of the Archishuttle guides, which give a lowdown on structures of interest according to tram and bus routes, enabling you to see the sights without being herded along with groups of tourists. Faced with zinc-coated aluminium, the curvy three-storey waterside HQ, designed by Almere-based René van Zuuk, cleverly incorporates an earlier small pavilion by Renzo Piano. It also operates as a useful meeting point. *Prins Hendrikkade 600, T 620 4878, www.arcam.nl*

Openbare Bibliotheek Amsterdam

The Netherlands' largest public library, welcoming about 6,000 visitors each day, Openbare Bibliotheek Amsterdam (OBA) boldly claims to be the hub of cultural life in the country. Opened in 2007, the project certainly has the credentials to back up such an assertion, consisting of a series of huge floors that house everything from a theatre to exhibition spaces, a comic-book archive and a restaurant, connected by an atrium of dizzying proportions, the work of chief government architect Jo Coenen. The dynamism within is evident from the interesting angles of the front elevation (above), where a distorted canopied square clad in light stone surrounds a raised five-storey bank of windows set in wood frames. Above this, the terrace has fantastic vistas.

Oosterdokskade 143, T 523 0900, www.oba.nl

SHOPS
THE BEST RETAIL THERAPY AND WHAT TO BUY

In a city that has more than 10,000 stores, any visitor with a sharp eye will return home laden with loot. The most popular retail area is The Nine Streets (De Negen Straatjes), which straddle the four main canals. In this strollable quarter, curiosity shops stand cheek-by-jowl with contemporary boutiques, and you can buy everything from high-end clothing at Rika (Oude Spiegelstraat 9, T 330 1112) to cheese at De Kaaskamer (Runstraat 7, T 623 3483) and art books at Mendo (Berenstraat 11, T 612 1216). Hazenstraat is dubbed 'The Tenth Street', thanks to enterprises such as Chocolátl (No 25a, T 789 3670) and, on its side roads, galleries including Stigter Van Doesburg (Elandstraat 90, T 624 2361) and Annet Gelink (Laurierstraat 187-189, T 330 2066). Rozengracht is crammed with interiors outlets, notably Raw Materials (No 229-233, T 421 3893), and seek out The Otherist (Leliegracht 6, T 320 0420), which is good for quirky gifts.

For upscale options, check out Cornelis Schuytstraat (see p088) in Oud Zuid, where you'll find multibrand womenswear, including Amsterdam-based British label Zoe Karssen, at VLVT (No 22 and 24, T 221 5256) and avant-garde fashion from Maison Margiela and Ann Demeulemeester, and many more, at Ennu (No 15, T 673 5265). Students and artists fill their apartments and wardrobes in De Pijp. The eco-savvy head to Charlie + Mary (Gerard Doustraat 84, T 662 8281) and Studio JUX (Ceintuurbaan 252, T 753 1843).

For full addresses, see Resources.

Marie-Stella-Maris

Founded by Patrick Munsters (see p088) and Carel Neuberg, this cosmetics label donates one Euro from each sale to clean-water projects in the developing world. The design motif in the flagship store is the text of UN Resolution 64/292, which is laid out in black and red on a lightbox that covers the back wall; elsewhere there is plenty of foliage and hanging fluorescent 'Mr Tubes' lamps by Tonone. The signature product is an olfactory tribute to its home city – No 92 Objets d'Amsterdam, a mix of white tea, lemon and bergamot, that comes as a scented candle and a room spray. The soaps and lotions are made using natural ingredients including jojoba and almond oils, lavender and geranium. Downstairs, a café serves coffee and branded water. *Keizersgracht 357, T 852 732 845, www.marie-stella-maris.com*

ETQ Store

This ultra-minimal space used to be the home of maximalist glam – the legendary Roxy club that introduced house music to Amsterdam before it burnt down in 1999. Various ill-fated retail concepts followed before local brand ETQ entered the fray in 2015. Initially a showcase for its pared-back 'seasonless' sneakers, such as the enduring 'Low 1' model, available (like most lines) in white, grey or black soft leather, the split-level space became multibrand after a conversion by Studio Jos van Dijk. Every last embellishment has been exhumed, the walls have been sandblasted, and metal cages and raw concrete slabs now display menswear from Phillip Lim, Études and ETQ's Store Merch range of monochrome sweats and tees. Also look out for shades by Dick Moby and TRNSPRNT bags.
Singel 465, T 261 3815, www.etqstore.com

Hutspot

This department store, housing a series of internal pop-ups, proved so successful at its original location in De Pijp that, in 2013, a second, larger venture was opened in a former distillery in Jordaan. The additional 800 sq m of space displays a mishmash of fashion, furniture, books and ceramics, by approximately 80 creative start-ups, from Design Letters' homewares to the self-explanatory Damn Good Soap. New lines debut every few weeks, and while Hutspot maintains a focus on local items, such as Majem's raincoat/biking poncho and Bone's porcelain pots, it has started to add more Scandi brands to the mix, like Samsøe & Samsøe and Monokel Eyeware. Unwind with a coffee in the on-site café in the company of the resident dog, Gumbo. *Rozengracht 204-210, T 370 8708, www.hutspot.com*

The Frozen Fountain

The gallery section of this store spans two floors, showcasing well-known designers such as Patricia Urquiola and the Eameses, but The Frozen Fountain is principally a hothouse for emerging homegrown talent. Piet Hein Eek and Marcel Wanders both launched their stellar careers here, so it's hallowed ground for every aspiring young Dutch creative. Traditional crafts are often reinterpreted and given a contemporary twist – the collaborative items are worth checking out, such as the 'Arita Porcelain Container' (above), €108, by Scholten & Baijings in conjunction with the Japanese porcelain manufacturer, and Dirk van der Kooij and Tel Aviv architects Baranowitz & Kronenberg's 'Sunflower' lamp, €3,685, which riffs on Van Gogh's floral leitmotif.
Prinsengracht 645, T 622 9375, www.frozenfountain.nl

ByAMFI

Many a venture claims to be a 'concept store', but ByAMFI goes the extra mile, with entire dreamscapes, like 'Washful Thinking', which transformed the space into a launderette using graphic screens, designed by second-year students at the city's renowned Fashion Institute (AMFI). Its location on the historic Spui square provides footfall for work made by third- and fourth-year undergraduates, subject to quality control by teaching staff, under the in-house Individuals brand, set up in 2006. Alumni include Mick Keus, who now has an atelier (T 633 056 919) reworking vintage denim into custom jeans, Daphny Raes, whose vegetable-tanned leather bags are on sale at Cotton Cake (see p092), and Tess van Zalinge, who debuted her lingerie lines and zoot-suit-inspired creations at Amsterdam Fashion Week in 2016. The venue often hosts events and launches.
Spui 23, T 525 8133, www.amfi.nl/byamfi

Salle Privée

No one could accuse Patrick Munsters of resting on his laurels after selling his stake in Scotch & Soda, the label he helped steer to high-street ubiquity. These days, he keeps his oar in at Marie-Stella-Maris (see p081) and Salle Privée, a menswear line that upscales the modern Dutch aesthetic. Refined Italian-made staples encompass wool overcoats, cotton-twill chinos, crisp Oxfords and smart suiting. It's a compact store, but the layout cleverly maximises display space, with stepped cantilevered platforms rising to a mezzanine on both sides flanking a marble staircase that leads down to accessories, more fashion and the sales counter. The interior is by Rotterdam-based designer Sabine Marcelis, who art-directed the brand's fragrance campaign. *Cornelis Schuytstraat 9, T 850 160 539, www.salle-privee.com*

X Bank

In his 1986 film *Abel*, Alex van Warmerdam used this building, formerly the HQ of the mighty Kas Bank, as visual shorthand for desolation and grinding bureaucracy. How times change. Now, it is the perky W Hotel and on its first floor, X Bank is a platform for 180 Dutch creatives. The national recipe for aesthetic endeavour – four parts sober minimalism to one part tongue-in-cheek quirk – seems to have been reversed here, with the suggestive, fluorescent fashion of local wunderkind Bas Kosters setting the trippy Mad Hatter-ish tone. There is ready-to-wear by couturier-to-the-queen Claes Iversen, and streetwear brand Daily Paper, plus lighting by Alex de Witte, and plenty of gift options, including Hermit, a coriander-infused craft gin from the coast. *Spuistraat 172, T 811 3320, www.xbank.amsterdam*

Misc
This store purveys beautiful stationery
from Scandinavia, Japan and Belgium,
such as Postalco iPad covers, Wms&Co
accessories and Traveler's notebooks.
Misc began online and a workshop ethos
prevails with wares displayed on desks,
cork boards and Vitsoe-esque shelving.
De Intuïtiefabriek ceramics and Atelier
Naerebout lamps are local offerings.
De Clercqstraat 130, T 700 9855

Cotton Cake

Jorinde Westhoff and Tessa van Herwijnen whitewashed the brick walls and painted the floorboards of their bijou boutique themselves, and its ethereal and rather twee aesthetic endures. A curated edit of womenswear features a roster of brands that changes each season; we picked up a leather shopper by local Daphny Raes and admired the handmade jewellery by Amsterdam-based Monocrafft. Artworks by the likes of Carlijn Claire Potma, who creates intricate pieces in artisanal paper using just pinpricks, are for sale. A coffee bar brews roasts from White Label, and upstairs, the café has a veg-centric menu and gluten-free cakes; the toasted walnut banana bread served with organic butter and raspberry rhubarb compote is a hit. *1e van der Helststraat 76, T 789 5838, www.cottoncake.nl*

Hôtel Droog

Renny Ramakers and Gijs Bakker launched their conceptual design brand in 1993. Its mothership is set within two 17th-century buildings styled as a 'hotel', where you can shop, eat, relax and sleep. There may be just one suite, minimally furnished with prototypes, but it is one of the city's most unique places to stay. A 'library' (above) of blank books can be hired for meetings and events, there's a courtyard garden, a café/bar, and a store with fashion by Dutch labels Iris van Herpen, Spijkers en Spijkers and Frenken. Plus, of course, Droog's witty pieces including 'Milk Bottle Lamp'; 'Fish Restaurant', a Chinese table setting for an aquarium; and the 'Do Hit Chair', a hollow stainless-steel cube, with a sledgehammer for the buyer to create their own seat. *Staalstraat 7b, T 523 5050, www.droog.com*

Ace & Tate

The name of this rising eyewear brand is a reference to acetate, the material from which its pleasingly fuss-free, lushly hued frames are made. By carrying out design, supply and distribution without middlemen and forgoing ad campaigns, founder Mark de Lange has ensured prices rarely stray into much above triple figures. Within a vintage-inspired formula are some modish styles, such as the rounded 'Jamie' specs and bold 'Yves' shades, both of which are unisex. There are collaborations too, such as a limited-edition set of mirrored 'rolling eyes' sunglasses by Lernert & Sander. The Haarlemmerstraat store, one of three (and counting) in the city, features wood floors and Bart de Baets' posters, inspired by the seminal graphic designer Willem Sandberg. *Haarlemmerstraat 70, T 261 8921, www.aceandtate.nl*

Matter of Material

Inspired by Thomas Eyck's project (his brand TE is sold here), and purity of form and craft, Arne Leliveld deals in design pieces that champion a specific material. Many speak intimately of their origin; others, like Margje Teeuwen and Erwin Zwiers' 'Proplamp', a non-woven-plastic amorphous light resembling scrunched paper, simply masquerade. Exclusives include Rotterdamer Lex Pott's Douglas fir room-divider, sandblasted to reveal the tree's growth pattern, and Hella Jongerius' glazed porcelain vases. Eindhoven-based Atelier NL's 'Savelsbos' carafe and tumbler set (above) is part of a series made using sand from different corners of the country. Located in the antiques quarter, the shop is pared back and flooded with natural light. *Kerkstraat 163, T 777 0707, www.matterofmaterial.com*

ESCAPES

WHERE TO GO IF YOU WANT TO LEAVE TOWN

As the Netherlands is such a tiny country (you can drive right across it in two hours), a day trip from Amsterdam throws up plenty of options. Art aficionados are completely spoilt for choice. In The Hague, a 50-minute train ride from Centraal Station, the yellow-brick Gemeentemuseum (Stadhouderslaan 41, T 070 338 1111), designed by architect Hendrik Petrus Berlage, has works by Monet, Mondrian, Picasso et al. Its acclaimed Mauritshuis (Plein 29, T 070 302 3456) reopened in 2014 after major renovation and, although the museum itself is relatively small, its collection is one of the most famous in the world. Its highlights are the masterpieces from the Golden Age, in particular Carel Fabritius' *The Goldfinch*, and Vermeer's *Girl with a Pearl Earring* and *View of Delft*, a haunting portrayal of his hometown. But there are now aesthetic treats right across Holland, due to the philanthropy of private Dutch collectors, who have founded destination art venues in Wassenaar (opposite), Gorssel (see p098) and De Hoge Veluwe National Park (see p102).

Haarlem is practically a suburb of Amsterdam, only 20 minutes by train, but it has a provincial feel in comparison, as well as buzzy beach clubs in nearby Bloemendaal (see p100). If you're looking for seclusion, head to De Echoput hotel (Amersfoortseweg 86, T 055 519 1248), an hour east close to Apeldoorn, which is set in a pretty forest and inspired by the work of Frank Lloyd Wright.

For full addresses, see Resources.

Museum Voorlinden, Wassenaar

Chemicals baron Joop van Caldenborgh established Clingenbosch sculpture park (T 070 512 1660) on his forested estate in 1995. Here, from May to October, guided walks take in more than 60 works by the likes of Henry Moore, Anish Kapoor, Sol LeWitt and Dutchman Joep van Lieshout. In 2016, Van Caldenborgh's collection was further opened up to the public thanks to Rotterdam architects Kraaijvanger's sleek single-storey pavilion (above) in an equally bucolic setting 1km away. Under a ground-breaking translucent glass canopied roof, 20 galleries show pieces by Richard Serra, Ellsworth Kelly and Andy Warhol, and site-specific installations such as James Turrell's *Skyspace* and Leandro Erlich's *Swimming Pool*. It is an hour's drive from the capital. *Buurtweg 90, T 070 512 1660, www.voorlinden.nl*

Museum More, Gorssel

In 2015, the financier Hans Melchers also opened his own museum, in Gorssel, two hours east of Amsterdam. Architects Hans van Heeswijk converted a 1914 town hall, adding three two-storey limestone-clad wings that extend out in sequence from a rebuilt glass entrance hall. It is dedicated to Dutch realism, stretching back 100 years to include Raoul Hynckes' melancholic still-lifes and Sal Meijer's charming Amsterdam-scapes, but also contemporary acquisitions from Marlene Dumas and Ruud van Empel. In 2017 Melchers unveiled a second venue, Kasteel Ruurlo (T 057 576 0300), an 18th-century moated castle half an hour away, masterfully adapted by Verlaan & Bouwstra to showcase 45 works by Carel Willink, who described his style as 'imaginary realism'. *Hoofdstraat 28, T 057 576 0300, www.museummore.nl/en*

Rietveld Schröder House, Utrecht

Widowed socialite Truus Schröder's brief when she commissioned Gerrit Rietveld in 1924 was for a modern abode that spoke of 'luxury in frugality'. It allowed him to emphatically realise the tenets of De Stijl. The two storeys hardly feature a curved line, terraces merge the interior/exterior divide, sliding panels open up the space or close off rooms, furniture is orthogonally arranged, and there is a strict Mondrian palette. Strikingly avant-garde even today, it was dubbed the 'crazy house' by one of Schröder's daughters, and condemned as impractical by Rietveld himself, who moved in with Schröder upon the death of his wife in a still-mysterious arrangement. Book a one-hour tour through Centraal Museum. The train trip to Utrecht takes half an hour. *Prins Hendriklaan 50, T 030 236 2362, www.centraalmuseum.nl/en*

Bloemendaal

The coolest stretch of coast in the country, Bloemendaal is a lure for Amsterdammers in search of sun, sand and sounds. To join them, take the train to Zandvoort, a more traditional seaside town, from where it's a 20-minute walk along the shore, or travel to Haarlem, then hop on a bus. From April through September, the beachfront is one long lounge bar/alfresco nightclub. Head for Republiek (above; T 023 573 0730), or wander down to the hippyish hangout Woodstock 69 (Zeeweg 7). For a different vibe, go north to see the kitesurfers at Wijk aan Zee, and the café Timboektoe (T 025 137 3050). Getting there isn't easy without a car, but cycling is an adventure through Een Zee Van Staal sculpture park. Once you are on the beach it's a surreal experience: sea in front, dunes and huge steel mill behind, and kites overhead.

Kröller-Müller Museum, Otterlo

Mining heiress Helene Kröller-Müller used her wealth to buy 11,500 artworks between 1907 and 1922, and was one of the first to recognise the talent of Van Gogh, amassing 300 paintings and drawings. She donated the collection and her land to the state, on the condition that a museum was realised in situ, and the austere result, designed by Henry van de Velde, was unveiled in 1938. A sculpture park added in 1961 saw Gerrit Rietveld's Sonsbeek Pavilion, created for the 1955 Arnhem expo, rebuilt here (above) to display a series by Barbara Hepworth. Elsewhere are pieces by other giants of the genre. Recent acquisitions have included contemporary Dutch talent like Joep van Lieshout. It's an hour's drive to the three entrances, where free bikes are on hand. *Houtkampweg 6, T 031 859 1241, www.krollermuller.nl/visit*

Almere

Before 1976, Almere didn't exist. Now, on reclaimed land half an hour's drive from Amsterdam, it is one of the Netherlands' fastest-growing sites. Work began in 1994 on the raised city centre, positioned over parking facilities and bus lanes below, and planned by OMA; Almere also boasts the work of Christian de Portzamparc, David Chipperfield, SANAA and UNStudio. SMC Alsop's 16,000 sq m Urban Entertainment Centre, completed in 2003, includes the Apollo Hotel (above; T 036 527 4500), with its amorphous brass-clad lobby and cedar-clad 'sleeping block'. The housing policy eschews cookie-cutter ubiquity in favour of individualism and has been lauded as an urban masterstroke, from the custom-builds at Almere Poort to the often wacky self-builds (to a set of design principles by MVRDV) in the suburb of Oosterwold.

NOTES

SKETCHES AND MEMOS

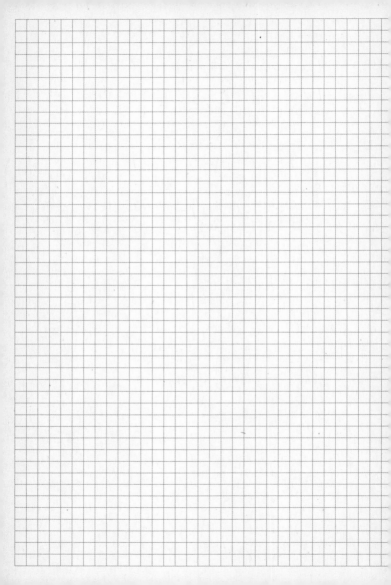

RESOURCES

CITY GUIDE DIRECTORY

HOTELS

ADDRESSES AND ROOM RATES

Amstel 016
Room rates:
double, from €420
Professor Tulpplein 1
T 622 6060
www.amsterdam.intercontinental.com

Andaz 016
Room rates:
double, from €295
Prinsengracht 587
T 523 1234
www.andaz.hyatt.com

Apollo Hotel 103
Room rates:
double, from €100
Koetsierbaan 2
Almere
T 036 527 4500
www.apollohotels.nl

Hotel Arena 016
Room rates:
double, from €170
's-Gravesandestraat 55
T 850 2400
www.hotelarena.nl

CitizenM 027
Room rates:
double, from €90
Prinses Irenestraat 30
T 811 7090
www.citizenm.com/destinations/
amsterdam/amsterdam-hotel

Conservatorium 017
Room rates:
double, from €620;
Grand Duplex Suite, from €870
Van Baerlestraat 27
T 570 0000
www.conservatoriumhotel.com

Hôtel Droog 093
Room rates:
double, from €255
Staalstraat 7b
T 523 5050
www.hoteldroog.com

The Dylan 024
Room rates:
double, from €325;
Loft Suite, from €775
Keizersgracht 384
T 530 2010
www.dylanamsterdam.com

De Echoput 096
Room rates:
double, from €100
Amersfoortseweg 86
Hoog Soeren
T 055 519 1248
www.echoput.nl

Hotel de l'Europe 016
Room rates:
double, from €340
Nieuwe Doelenstraat 2-14
T 531 1777
www.deleurope.com

The Grand 016
Room rates:
double, from €325
Oudezijds Voorburgwal 197
T 555 3111
www.sofitel.com

The Hoxton 018
Room rates:
double, from €130;
Floral Room 107, from €160
Herengracht 255
T 888 5555
www.thehoxton.com/amsterdam

Lloyd Hotel 016
Room rates:
double, from €75
Oostelijke Handelskade 34
T 561 3636
www.lloydhotel.com

Maison Rika 030
Room rates:
Loft Room, from €210;
View Room, from €210
Oude Spiegelstraat 12
T 330 1112
www.rikastudios.com/maison

Marcel's Creative Exchange 016
Room rates:
double, from €200
Leidsestraat 87
T 622 9834
www.marcelamsterdam.nl

Pulitzer 026
Room rates:
double, from €270;
Art Collector's Suite, from €800;
Book Collector's Suite, from €800
Prinsengracht 315-331
T 523 5235
www.pulitzeramsterdam.com

Sir Adam 020
Room rates:
double, from €190;
Sir Suite 711, from €575
Overhoeksplein 7
T 215 9500
www.sirhotels.com/adam

Sir Albert 016
Room rates:
double, from €160
Albert Cuypstraat 2-6
T 305 3020
www.sirhotels.com/albert

Stout & Co 029
Room rates:
suite, from €150;
Mixed Green, from €150
Hoogte Kadijk 71
T 220 9071
www.stout-co.com

Hotel V Fizeaustraat 022
Room rates:
double, from €150;
Suite, from €230
Fizeaustraat 2
T 662 3233
www.hotelvfizeaustraat.nl

Hotel V Frederiksplein 022
Room rates:
double, from €90
Weteringschans 136
T 662 3233
www.hotelvfrederiksplein.nl

Hotel V Nesplein 022
Room rates:
double, from €110
Nes 49
T 662 3233
www.hotelvnesplein.nl

Waldorf Astoria 016
Room rates:
double, from €410
Herengracht 542-556
T 710 6090
www.waldorfastoria.com

Zoku 028
Room rates:
double, from €100;
XL, from €150
Weesperstraat 105
T 811 2811
www.livezoku.com

WALLPAPER* CITY GUIDES

Executive Editor
Jeremy Case

Author
Mark Smith

Deputy Editor
Belle Place

Photography Editor
Rebecca Moldenhauer

Junior Art Editor
Jade R Arroyo

Editorial Assistant
Charlie Monaghan

Contributors
Steve Korver
Daniëlle Siobhán Mol
Alex Onderwater
Marta Bausells

Interns
Nicole Alber
Jonny Clowes
Sasha Mather

Amsterdam Imprint
First published 2006
Eighth edition 2018

ISBN 978 0 7148 7478 4

More City Guides
www.phaidon.com/travel

Follow Us
@wallpaperguides

Contact
wcg@phaidon.com

Original Design
Loran Stosskopf
Map Illustrator
Russell Bell

Production Controllers
Zuzana Cimalova
Gif Jittiwutikarn

Wallpaper* Magazine
161 Marsh Wall
London E14 9AP
contact@wallpaper.com

Editor-in-Chief
Tony Chambers

Wallpaper*® is a
registered trademark
of Time Inc (UK)

Phaidon Press Limited
Regent's Wharf
All Saints Street
London N1 9PA

Phaidon Press Inc
65 Bleecker Street
New York, NY 10012

All prices and venue
information are correct
at time of going to press,
but are subject to change.

A CIP Catalogue record for
this book is available from
the British Library.

PHOTOGRAPHERS

Luuk Kramer
The Whale, p012
NEMO, p013
Sir Adam, p021
Zoku, p028
Stout & Co, p029
Maison Rika, pp030-031
Bocca, p033
Stedelijk Museum,
pp036-037
De Kas, pp038-039
De Tropen, pp042-043
CT Coffee and Coconuts,
p044, p045
Choux, p046
C Amsterdam, p047
Café Panache, p050
Restaurant Anna, p051
SLA, pp052-053
Strangelove in
LAB111, p054
Hangar, p055
Morgan & Mees,
pp056-057
De Culinaire
Werkplaats, p058
Wilde Zwijnen, pp060-061
Andrea Trimarchi and
Simone Farresin, p063

Galerie Fons Welters,
pp068-069
Cuyperspassage, p070
EYE, p073
De Piramides, p074
Hope, Love and
Fortune, p075
Floating Houses, IJburg,
pp076-077
Openbare Bibliotheek
Amsterdam, p079
Marie-Stella-Maris, p081
ETQ Store, pp082-083
Hutspot, p084
ByAMFI, pp086-087
Salle Privée, p088
X Bank, p089
Misc, pp090-091
Hôtel Droog, p093
Museum More, p098

**Amsterdam Tourism
& Convention Board**
Amsterdam city view,
inside front cover

Thomas Eyck
Arita Porcelain
Container, p085

Amit Geron
Conservatorium, p017

Getty Images
Van Gogh Museum,
pp014-015

Walter Herfst
Kröller-Müller
Museum, p102

Ewout Huibers
CitizenM, p027

Ernst Moritz
Rietveld Schröder
House, p099

Pedro Pegenaute
Rijksmuseum, p035

Alex Prior
The Hoxton, pp018-019

Wim Ruigrok
ARCAM, p078

AMSTERDAM
A COLOUR-CODED GUIDE TO THE HOT 'HOODS

DE PIJP
A dynamic district with a busy market, one-off boutiques and Amsterdam School houses

WESTERPARK
Converting a gasworks into a cultural complex has rejuvenated this once-rundown area

CENTRUM
Avoid the sleaze and the stag parties, and instead enjoy the upmarket shopping here

JORDAAN
Cool cafés, hip bars and beautiful people inhabit one of the most happening parts of town

HAVENS OOST
The site of an ambitious docks regeneration scheme that actually seems to have worked

OUD ZUID
Now more than just a museum quarter, the city's first suburb is staging a chic comeback

For a full description of each neighbourhood, see the Introduction.
Featured venues are colour-coded, according to the district in which they are located.